Greta Thunberg

I know this to be true

on truth,
courage &
saving our planet

Interview and photography
Geoff Blackwell

CHRONICLE BOOKS
SAN FRANCISCO

in association with

Blackwell&Ruth.

Dedicated to the legacy
and memory of
Nelson Mandela

'People always tell us that they are so hopeful. They are hopeful that the young people are going to save the world. But we are not. There is simply not enough time to wait for us to grow up and become the ones in charge.'

Introduction

In August 2018, Greta Thunberg rode her bike to the Swedish parliament in Stockholm and sat on the cobblestones outside with a handmade sign reading '*skolstrejk för klimatet*' (School Strike for Climate). Pamphlets stating 'I am doing this because you adults are shitting on my future'[1] sat at her feet. She was fifteen. She was angry.

That summer had been Sweden's hottest since records began over two hundred and sixty years ago.[2] The world was warming at an alarming rate. The planet was suffering the drastic effects of climate change at a volume far greater than ever before. The human race was facing the defining issue of its time, and yet no one seemed to be doing anything about it. Things had to change – and they had to change fast. Thunberg wanted the Swedish government to reduce carbon emissions according to the Paris Agreement.[i]

It all began when she entered a climate writing competition for the Swedish newspaper *Svenska Dagbladet* earlier in the year. When her essay "We know – and we can do something now" was announced as one of the winning entries,[3] she gained her first media attention. A fellow climate activist suggested she look to the students at Marjory Stoneman Douglas High School in Florida, USA, who skipped school to protest gun violence in the wake of a mass shooting. She was inspired. As a student, refusing to attend school was an effective way to draw attention to her cause.

That first day outside parliament she sat alone with her sign, her pamphlets and a packed lunch. She stayed for the full school day, from 8.30 a.m. to 3 p.m., and posted her activity on social media. During the first strike she was approached by local journalists, and when she returned the next day other people began to join her. Business professionals, politicians, tourists and ordinary people viewed the protest as they passed by, and the word spread quickly.

Stories about her efforts began to surface on major news outlets. When *The Guardian* published an article called "The Swedish 15-year-old who's cutting class to fight the climate crisis"[4] just eleven days after Thunberg began striking, the floodgates opened. She was asked to speak at a People's Climate

March rally[ii] in front of thousands of people. Some filmed her and shared it on social media. Soon she had tens of thousands, then hundreds of thousands, of followers.

Every day for three weeks she maintained her post, rain or shine, and despite her parents' initial disapproval. (Both are now fully supportive of their daughter, and have adopted mostly vegetarian diets and cut back on air travel.) Unsatisfied with the outcome of the Swedish general election, Thunberg resolved to resume striking on Fridays. 'I will go on with the school strike', she wrote on social media. 'Every Friday as from now I will sit outside the Swedish parliament until Sweden is in line with the Paris agreement. I urge all of you to do the same. . . . Time is much shorter than we think. Failure means disaster.'[5]

Thunberg learned of the realities of climate change when she was eight. She was horrified that no one – including adults – seemed to take it seriously. After discovering just how grave the planet's future was, she became depressed. She stopped going to school, stopped eating and stopped talking. She was later diagnosed with Asperger syndrome, obsessive-compulsive disorder and selective mutism. The latter meant that she only spoke when necessary – and when it came to the climate crisis, for Thunberg it was necessary.

Her resolve deepened when a 2018 report by the UN Intergovernmental Panel on Climate Change (IPCC)[iii] found that global temperatures were rising more rapidly than expected and could pass 1.5 degrees Celsius global warming, bringing extreme consequences to the planet – rising waters, increased natural disasters and mass extinction just some of the inevitable outcomes.[6] She decided to make it her personal mission to bring to light the reality of this ever-looming climate crisis fallout.

Just a few months after she first sat down outside Swedish parliament, Thunberg's name and face was known around the world. Addressing crowds at major climate meetings – including the 2019 World Economic Forum[iv] and the 2019 UN Climate Action Summit[v] – she called on people to unite behind the wealth of climate change science. Forthright and unapologetic, she challenged political figures and lawmakers to use their position to enact change. But while those in power should be doing more, Thunberg's own actions proved that every person is responsible.

Already her steadfast activism has made an irrevocable mark. Her school strikes have mobilized students in more than one hundred and fifty countries around the globe to hold protests of their own, culminating in a Global Climate Strike for Future which saw over 7 million youth take to the streets.[7]

In 2019 she embarked on a two-week journey across the Atlantic Ocean aboard a sixty-foot zero-emission racing yacht to attend the United Nations (UN) Climate Action Summit in New York, USA. A large crowd greeted her on arrival, and with her feet safely on land she joined hundreds of youth in a mass protest outside the UN headquarters. Holding her '*skolstrejk för klimatet*' sign she sat in the middle of the rally, surrounded by her American supporters with a single demand: urgent action on the climate crisis.

The moment proved Thunberg's far-reaching influence. Her defiance is the seed that planted the international youth movement against climate change – arguably the most important movement the planet has encountered – and is proof that a single person really can create meaningful change.

But her journey as a climate change activist is far from over. Transformation is underway, but progress is slow. Generating awareness may be easier in the age of social media, but fostering belief is more difficult. Many doubt the facts provided by scientific research, and Thunberg has come under personal attack from climate change sceptics and critics. Yet rather than deterring her, it has only strengthened her resolve. 'I have promised myself that I'm going to do everything I can for as long as I can,' she says.[8]

'What we do or don't do right now, me and my generation can't undo in the future.'

Prologue

My name is Greta Thunberg, I am sixteen years old and I'm from Sweden.

I have a dream: that governments, political parties and corporations grasp the urgency of the climate and ecological crisis and come together despite their differences – as you would in an emergency – and take the measures required to safeguard the conditions for a dignified life for everybody on earth.

Because then, we millions of school striking youth could go back to school.

I have a dream that the people in power, as well as the media, start treating this crisis like the existential emergency it is. So that I could go home to my sister and my dogs. Because I miss them.

In fact I have many dreams. But this is the year 2020. This is not the time and place for dreams. This is the time to wake up. This is the moment in history when we need to be wide awake.

And yes, we need dreams, we cannot live without dreams. But there's a time and place for everything. And dreams cannot stand in the way of telling it like it is.

And yet, wherever I go I seem to be surrounded by fairy tales. Business leaders, elected officials all across the political spectrum spending their time making up and telling bedtime stories that soothe us, that make us go back to sleep.

These are 'feel-good' stories about how we are going to fix everything. How wonderful everything is going to be when we have 'solved' everything. But the problem we are facing is not that we lack the ability to dream, or to imagine a better world. The problem now is that we need to wake up. It's time to face the reality, the facts, the science.

And the science doesn't mainly speak of 'great opportunities to create the society we always wanted'. It tells of unspoken human sufferings, which will get worse and worse the longer we delay action – unless we start to act now. And yes, of course a sustainable transformed world will include lots of new benefits. But you have to understand. This is not primarily an opportunity to create new green jobs, new businesses or green economic growth. This is above all an emergency, and not just any emergency. This is the biggest crisis humanity has ever faced.

And we need to treat it accordingly so that people can understand and grasp the urgency. Because you cannot solve a crisis without treating it as one. Stop telling people that everything will be fine when in fact, as it looks now, it won't be very fine. This is not something you can package and sell or 'like' on social media.

Stop pretending that you, your business idea, your political party or plan will solve everything. We must realize that we don't have all the solutions yet. Far from it. Unless those solutions mean that we simply stop doing certain things.

Changing one disastrous energy source for a slightly less disastrous one is not progress. Exporting our emissions overseas is not reducing our emission. Creative accounting will not help us. In fact, it's the very heart of the problem.

Some of you may have heard that we have twelve years from 1 January 2018 to cut our emissions of carbon dioxide in half. But I guess that hardly any of you have heard that there is a 50 per cent chance of staying below 1.5 degrees Celsius of global temperature rise above pre-industrial levels. Fifty per cent chance.[9]

'We need to cooperate and work together and share the resources of the planet in a new way. We need to start living within the planetary boundaries, focus on equity and take a few steps back for the sake of all living species. We need to protect the biosphere, the air, the oceans, the soil, the forests.'

And these current, best available scientific calculations do not include non-linear tipping points as well as most unforeseen feedback loops like the extremely powerful methane gas escaping from rapidly thawing arctic permafrost. Or already locked in warming hidden by toxic air pollution. Or the aspect of equity; climate justice.

So a 50 per cent chance – a statistical flip of a coin – will most definitely not be enough. That would be impossible to morally defend. Would any one of you step onto a plane if you knew it had more than a 50 per cent chance of crashing? More to the point: would you put your children on that flight?

And why is it so important to stay below the 1.5 degrees limit? Because that is what the united science calls for, to avoid destabilising the climate, so that we stay clear of setting off an irreversible chain reaction beyond human control. Even at 1 degree of warming we are seeing an unacceptable loss of life and livelihoods.

So where do we begin? Well I would suggest that we start looking at Chapter 2, on page 108 in the IPCC report that came out last year. Right there it says that if we are to have a 67 per cent chance of limiting the global temperature rise to below 1.5 degrees Celsius, we had, on 1 January 2018, about four hundred twenty gigatonnes of CO_2 left to emit in that carbon dioxide budget.[10] And of course that number is much lower today. As we emit about forty-two gigatonnes of CO_2 every year, if you include land use.[11]

With today's emissions levels, that remaining budget is gone within less than eight and a half years. These numbers are not my opinions. They aren't anyone's opinions or political views. This is the current best available science. Though a great number of scientists suggest even these figures are too moderate, these are the ones that have been accepted by all nations through the IPCC.

And please note that these figures are global and therefore do not say anything about the aspect of equity, clearly stated throughout the Paris Agreement, which is absolutely necessary to make it work on a global scale. That means that richer countries need to do their fair share and get down to zero emissions much faster, so that people in poorer countries can heighten their standard of living, by building some of the infrastructure that we have already built. Such as roads, hospitals, schools, clean drinking water and electricity.

Four hundred and twenty gigatonnes of CO_2 left to emit on 1 January 2018 to have a 67 per cent chance of staying below 1.5 degrees of global temperature rise.[12] Now that figure is already down to less than 360 gigatonnes.

These numbers are very uncomfortable. But people have the right to know. And the vast majority of us have no idea these numbers even exist. In fact not even the journalists that I meet seem to know that they even exist. Not to mention the politicians. And yet they all seem so certain that their political plan will solve the entire crisis.

But how can we solve a problem that we don't even fully understand? How can we leave out the full picture and the current best available science?

I believe there is a huge danger in doing so. And no matter how political the background to this crisis may be, we must not allow this to continue to be a partisan political question. The climate and ecological crisis is beyond party politics. And our main enemy right now is not our political opponents. Our main enemy now is physics. And we cannot make 'deals' with physics.

Everybody says that making sacrifices for the survival of the biosphere – and to secure the living conditions for future and present generations – is an impossible thing to do.

Perhaps it is impossible. But looking at those numbers – looking at the current best available science signed by every nation – then I think that is precisely what we are up against.

But you must not spend all of your time dreaming, or see this as some political fight to win.

And you must not gamble your children's future on the flip of a coin.

Instead, you must unite behind the science.

You must take action.

You must do the impossible.

Because giving up can never ever be an option.

From address to the United States Congress, September 2019

'It was only the second day when I was striking, someone joined me. And then another one.

That was an amazing feeling, I think everyone should have the opportunity to get that feeling. That you are actually capable of making a difference.'

The Interview

Who are you?

My name is Greta Thunberg. I am sixteen years old and I am from Sweden. I live in Stockholm, and I am a climate and environmental activist.

I think my concern about the environment and the climate began in school, when I was maybe eight or nine years old. I saw and heard these horrible stories about what humans had done to the environment, and what we were doing to the climate, that the climate was changing. I saw these horrifying pictures, and I just thought that this is horrible. Why aren't we doing everything we can to prevent this? And I just couldn't understand how we could just continue not caring about this.

So I started to read about it, and to learn. I talked to people and I eventually understood the seriousness of the crisis. Then I tried to convince my parents that this was actually happening. They were in a bit of denial, like, 'No, it's fine. Someone will come up with something.' And so on. And I became depressed. I saw that everything was just so wrong, and nothing mattered. How I got out of that depression was by thinking to myself, 'I can do so much, one person can do so much. And so I should try to do everything I can to change things, instead of just doing nothing.'

I promised myself that I was going to do everything I could to try to stop this. I tried to do that. And so I started school-striking for the climate. I was so desperate that nothing was happening and I just felt like someone needs to do something, and that someone could be me. I said to myself, 'I'm going to try this, and it might not work.' So I just sat down. And then it just got really big.

Where did the attention first come from? How did you manage to create the attention for your mission?

I don't know. The first thing I did when I started the school-strike was to post that I was school-striking on social media. It spread to a lot of people and some journalists started coming to me and interviewing me where I sat. And then more journalists started coming, and it became a thing in Sweden. It went viral. And then some people started to join me. It was only the second day when I was striking, someone joined me. And then another one.

That was an amazing feeling. I think everyone should have the opportunity to get that feeling. That you are actually capable of making a difference. The step from one to two is always the hardest, and once you have passed that step you're not far from creating movement.

And then it started spreading to other Swedish cities, and then to other countries – other children started school-striking – and then to other continents. I think one tipping point was when Australia started school-striking for the climate in November 2018, and there were tens of thousands of children on the streets marching. And then it spread to other countries, it became very big in other countries. And then I don't know what happened.

'The climate crisis has already been solved. We already have all the facts and the solutions. All we have to do is wake up and change.'

What really matters to you?

I think everything matters. And that is because everything we do matters, and that is why we have to really make a change in every way of our daily lives. Not just about the environment, but the way we treat other people, and the way we see life.

What matters to me in the climate crisis is that once we pass a certain point, it might be too late. Because then the earth starts warming itself – there are tipping points. For me, I always want routines and schedules, and I want to know what is happening. And I think that is one of the most scary parts of the climate crisis – that we don't know what the future looks like. Anything could happen, good or bad.

If you could effect real and fast change, what would it be?

The first thing I would do is to make people aware of what is going on, to make people aware of the situation. I think that once people fully know about this crisis, once people fully understand, they will change. They will care about this.

We need to start treating the crisis as a crisis, because we can't solve an emergency without treating it as an emergency. There are so incredibly many things you could do on a political level, so it's hard to mention, but I will just say that we must inform people and create international opinion. Because if enough people are pushing for change, then that change will happen.

And I would make people not be greedy. And make people realize that this is actually something that is happening, and it's because of us. Not every one of us, but at least, each one of us can do something about it.

What do you think the world needs more of now?

The world needs more people who care, and who want to make a difference. Now people say, 'Oh, this problem is too distant.' Or, 'There's nothing I can do.' Or, 'If there is anything I can do, it's already too late anyways.' That's one of the most common excuses I hear, 'Oh, I want to get involved in this, but it's already too late. I should have done it five years ago.'

But it's never too late to do as much as you can. What people don't understand is that today, it's so incredibly few people – if you see it from a big perspective – who actually are fighting for this, and who are actually aware of what is happening. If you start now, then you are one of the first ones.

How do you overcome challenges?

Not going to school was a problem in the beginning, definitely. Both because of my parents and my teachers, who were always telling me, 'You have to go to school.' But it just became a habit for me.

Did anyone say, 'Who do you think you are?'

Yes, all the time. All the time. Yes.

And you just said, 'This is what I'm doing?'

Yes, because I'm very stubborn. When I am fully passionate about something, then I really commit to it. And once I decide to do something I fulfil it.

Do you feel this is something you are going to be doing for a long time?

Unfortunately, yes. I say unfortunately because not enough action is being taken. I would love to stop doing this, because that would mean everything is fixed. But unfortunately it doesn't work that way.

Do you feel it's overtaking your life to some extent?

Yeah.

Do you have a particular aspiration or goal that you're working towards?

I have just said I'm going to do as much as I can, while I can. Of course, we children who are school-striking are saying that we are doing this until the world is in line with the Paris Agreement. And we are always only referring to the scientists and to the science. That is the thing we are striking for.

Do you know how many countries now are having school-strikes?

The last time I checked it was one hundred and sixty-five countries on all continents, including Antarctica.

Do you have guiding principles or a driving philosophy that underpin your life and decisions?

I just say that I'm doing what I think is right. If I say something, then I fully commit to it. I don't compromise. If I say I'm going to do this, then I don't make excuses and say I could do it another time. I really do it. I just have to say I'm doing what is right, and that, I think, is enough.

Do you feel the support of your contemporaries, the comments on social media for example? Does that help motivate you and make you feel like you're part of a collective movement?

Yes, because I think that one thing that makes you feel powerless is that you don't see anyone else who is passionate about the same things. I can see now that I'm not the only one who cares about this. Before I started school-striking, I thought that young people are just lazy, that we don't care about anything but ourselves. But then I was proven wrong.

Are you feeling support from older people?

Yes, many. I'm always told, 'Thank you, we support you.' And that is very good to hear, even if you hear it often, it's always comforting. That makes you feel happy.

'The one thing we need more than hope is action. Once we start to act, hope is everywhere. So instead of looking for hope, look for action. Then, and only then, hope will come.'

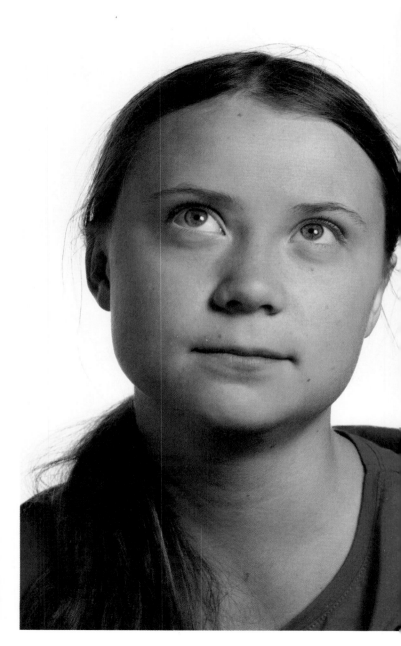

'I think the lowest depth of misery is when you're too depressed to see that you yourself actually matter.'

Is there a particular action that you want to
see from that generation that has the power to
actually implement real change? Are you seeing
real action?

To some extent, some. The children school-
striking, we are planning to have general
strikes, and adults are also striking so that
it's not only up to the children. Because it
shouldn't be that way. It shouldn't be the
children who take the responsibility. So now
we ask for help from the older generations
as well.

Has there been a special individual or individuals
that have particularly inspired you by their
example or wisdom?

All the time, yes of course. I am inspired by
people who really are making a difference, and
who are really committed to these things. The
leaders who gave me the inspiration to begin
this in the first place.

I think those individuals who inspire me
the most right now are those who are school-
striking, or striking from their work, in places
and in countries where they are not allowed

to protest and do these things. And they do it anyway. That is so moving and inspiring.

What does leadership mean to you?

Leadership means that you dare to take decisions that are for the greater good, and that you don't only see for yourself but for everyone; that you see what is best for everyone, and that you dare to be uncomfortable in saying uncomfortable things if necessary. And to not only see yourself.

What makes you happy?

My dogs make me happy! And when something is happening – like when change is coming, or happening. For example, when I see children school-striking, that makes me happy. To look through the Internet and just see millions of children who are school-striking for the climate – that makes me happy as well.

What do you regard as the lowest depth
of misery?

When you're too depressed to see that
you yourself actually matter.

You've been there?

Yes.

How did you find the strength to come out
of that?

It happened gradually. It was a lot thanks to
the climate and ecological crisis; I thought
that I need to do something and I can't just
sit here. It was the thing that got me into the
depression in the first place, but it was also
the thing that got me out of depression.

Are you supported? Are your parents
activist-types?

Before I became aware of the climate crisis,
they were just like everyone else. They
were frequent flyers, and they had huge
carbon footprints, and they lived high-carbon

lifestyles, and so on. I think they were as far from activists as you can come. But then I started talking about these things, and I talked about them all the time. I just kept on going, showing them the graphs, and the pictures and the reports, and they were like, 'Yeah, everything's gonna be fine.' And I just said, 'No, how can you say that?' Eventually they actually started to understand what I was saying, and then they took a few years to really understand. I think now they understand. They are still sometimes like, 'Yeah, but . . .' But they're getting there. I'm trying to turn them over.

What is your hope for your generation?

I hope that my generation will be very pushy, and actually very annoying. That we will annoy the older generation so much that they will have to do something. I know that I will never stop doing this and I just hope that others feel the same, so that we together can turn over the older generations.

'Adults keep saying, "We owe it to the young people to give them hope". But I don't want your hope. I don't want you to be hopeful. I want you to panic. I want you to feel the fear I feel every day, and then I want you to act. I want you to act as you would in a crisis. I want you to act as if our house is on fire. Because it is.'

Epilogue

According to the IPCC, we are less than twelve years away from not being able to undo our mistakes. In that time, unprecedented changes in all aspects of society need to have taken place, including a reduction of our CO_2 emissions by at least 50 per cent.

At places like Davos, people like to tell success stories. But their financial success has come with an unthinkable price tag. And on climate change, we have to acknowledge we have failed. All political movements in their present form have done so, and the media has failed to create broad public awareness.

But *Homo sapiens* have not yet failed.

Yes, we are failing, but there is still time to turn everything around. We can still fix this. We still have everything in our own hands. But unless we recognize the overall failures of our current systems, we most probably don't stand a chance.

We are facing a disaster of unspoken sufferings for enormous amounts of people. And now is not the time for speaking politely or focusing on what we can or cannot say. Now is the time to speak clearly.

Solving the climate crisis is the greatest and most complex challenge that *Homo sapiens* have ever faced. The main solution, however, is so simple that even a small child can understand it. We have to stop our emissions of greenhouse gases.

Either we do that or we don't.

You say nothing in life is black or white. But that is a lie. A very dangerous lie. Either we prevent 1.5 degrees Celsius of warming or we don't. Either we avoid setting off that irreversible chain reaction beyond human control or we don't.

Either we choose to go on as a civilisation or we don't. That is as black or white as it gets. There are no grey areas when it comes to survival.

We all have a choice. We can create transformational action that will safeguard the living conditions for future generations. Or we can continue with our business as usual and fail.

That is up to you and me.

Some say we should not engage in activism. Instead we should leave everything to our politicians and just vote for a change instead. But what do we do when there is no political will? What do we do when the politics needed are nowhere in sight?

And since the climate crisis has never once been treated as a crisis, people are simply not aware of the full consequences on our everyday life. People are not aware that there is such a thing as a carbon budget, and just how incredibly small that remaining carbon budget is. That needs to change today.

No other current challenge can match the importance of establishing a wide public awareness and understanding of our rapidly disappearing carbon budget, which should and must become our new global currency and the very heart of our future and present economics.

We are at a time in history where everyone with any insight of the climate crisis that threatens our civilisation – and the entire biosphere – must speak out in clear language, no matter how uncomfortable and unprofitable that may be.

We must change almost everything in our current societies. The bigger your carbon footprint, the bigger your moral duty. The bigger your platform, the bigger your responsibility.

'I am inspired by people who really are making a difference, and who are really committed to these things. The leaders who gave me the inspiration to begin this in the first place.'

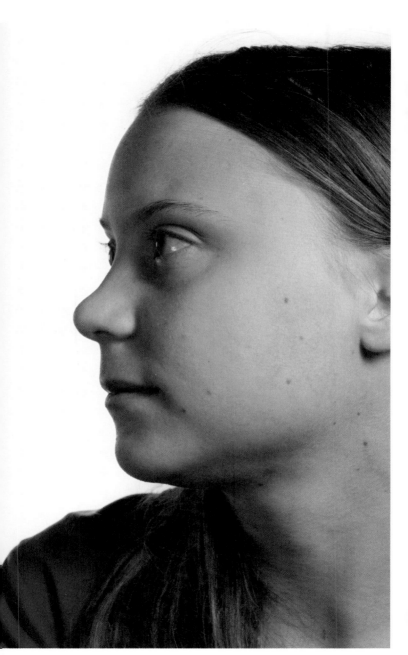

Adults keep saying, 'We owe it to the young people to give them hope.' But I don't want your hope. I don't want you to be hopeful. I want you to panic. I want you to feel the fear I feel every day. And then I want you to act.

I want you to act as you would in a crisis. I want you to act as if our house is on fire. Because it is.

From a speech at the World Economic Forum Annual Meeting, Davos-Klosters, Switzerland, January 2019

'Some people say that we are fighting for our future. But that is not true. We are not fighting for our future; we are fighting for everyone's future.'

About Greta Thunberg

Greta Thunberg is a teenage climate change activist from Sweden. When she was eight, she stopped attending school due to depression triggered from learning about global warming. A few years later she was diagnosed with Asperger syndrome, selective mutism and obsessive-compulsive disorder.

In August 2018, after Sweden's hottest summer in more than two hundred and sixty years,[13] Thunberg – then fifteen – decided to go on a school-strike for the climate. She was inspired by teenage activists in Florida, USA, who refused to attend school in the aftermath of the Marjory Stoneman Douglas High School shooting earlier in the year. Thunberg began protesting outside the Swedish parliament to demand action on the climate crisis, specifically calling upon the government to reduce national carbon emissions according to the recommendations outlined in the Paris Agreement.

Thunberg went on strike every day until the Swedish general election in September 2018, after which she resumed striking, on Fridays only. She then expanded her activism, participating in demonstrations across Europe and speaking at climate seminars and rallies including TEDxStockholm; the COP24 United Nations climate change summit in Katowice, Poland; and the World Economic Forum in Davos-Klosters, Switzerland.

Continuing her school-strikes, Thunberg's initiative has spread into a worldwide movement called Fridays For Future that has mobilized hundreds of thousands of school children. In September 2019, over 7 million people in one hundred and twenty-eight countries participated in a global climate strike.[14]

To maintain a low-carbon lifestyle, Thunberg is vegan and does not fly, typically travelling by train within Europe. In 2019 she sailed from the UK to the USA on a sixty-foot zero-emission racing yacht to attend the United Nations Climate Action Summit in New York, USA. The crossing took two weeks.

She has been acknowledged with numerous global recognitions, including being named one of *Time* magazine's Next Generation Leaders and 100 Most Influential People of 2019, receiving Amnesty International's Ambassador of Conscience Award, the Fritt Ords Prize for Freedom of Expression and the title of the Swedish Women's Educational Association Woman of the Year 2019. In 2019, she was nominated for a Nobel Peace Prize.

@gretathunberg

About the Project

'A true leader must work hard to ease tensions, especially when dealing with sensitive and complicated issues. Extremists normally thrive when there is tension, and pure emotion tends to supersede rational thinking.'

– Nelson Mandela

Inspired by Nelson Mandela, *I Know This to Be True* was conceived to record and share what really matters for the most inspiring leaders of our time.

I Know This to Be True is a Nelson Mandela Foundation project anchored by original interviews with twelve different and extraordinary leaders each year, for five years – six men and six women – who are helping and inspiring others through their ideas, values and work.

Royalties from sales of this book will support language translation and free access to films, books and educational programmes using material from the series, in all countries with developing economies, or economies in transition, as defined by United Nations annual classifications.

iknowthistobetrue.org

'A good head and a good
heart are always a formidable
combination.'

– Nelson Mandela

A special thanks to Greta Thunberg, and all the generous and inspiring individuals we call leaders who have magnanimously given their time to be part of this project.

For the Nelson Mandela Foundation:
Sello Hatang, Verne Harris, Noreen Wahome, Razia Saleh and Sahm Venter

For Blackwell & Ruth:
Geoff Blackwell, Ruth Hobday, Cameron Gibb, Nikki Addison, Olivia van Velthooven, Elizabeth Blackwell, Kate Raven, Annie Cai and Tony Coombe

We hope that together we can help to mobilize Madiba's extraordinary legacy, to the benefit of communities around the world.

A note from the photographer

The photographic portraits in this book are the result of a team effort, led by Blackwell & Ruth's talented design director Cameron Gibb, who both mentored and saved this fledgling photographer. I have long harboured the desire, perhaps conceit, that I could personally create photographs for one of our projects, but through many trials, and more than a few errors, I learned that without Cameron's generous direction and sensitivity, I couldn't have come close to creating these portraits. I would also like to acknowledge the on-the-ground support of Mark Dexter for helping me capture these images of Greta Thunberg.

– Geoff Blackwell

About Nelson Mandela

Nelson Mandela was born in the Transkei, South Africa, on 18 July 1918. He joined the African National Congress in the early 1940s and was engaged in struggles against the ruling National Party's apartheid system for many years before being arrested in August 1962. Mandela was incarcerated for more than twenty-seven years, during which his reputation as a potent symbol of resistance for the anti-apartheid movement grew steadily. Released from prison in 1990, Mandela was jointly awarded the Nobel Peace Prize in 1993, and became South Africa's first democratically elected president in 1994. He died on 5 December 2013, at the age of ninety-five.

NELSON MANDELA
FOUNDATION
Living the legacy

About the Nelson Mandela Foundation

The Nelson Mandela Foundation is a non-profit organization founded by Nelson Mandela in 1999 as his post-presidential office. In 2007 he gave it a mandate to promote social justice through dialogue and memory work.

Its mission is to contribute to the making of a just society by mobilizing the legacy of Nelson Mandela, providing public access to information on his life and times and convening dialogue on critical social issues.

The Foundation strives to weave leadership development into all aspects of its work.

nelsonmandela.org

Notes

i   Signed in Paris, France, on 12 December 2015, the Paris Agreement builds upon the UNFCCC (United Nations Framework Convention on Climate Change) with a stated central aim to strengthen the global response to the threat of climate change by keeping a global temperature rise this century below 2 degrees Celsius, and to pursue efforts to limit the temperature increase even further to 1.5 degrees Celsius.

ii   The People's Climate March was a protest which took place on Washington, D.C.'s National Mall together with other locations in the USA and around the world on 29 April 2017, to protest the environmental policies of US President Donald Trump's administration.

iii   The Intergovernmental Panel on Climate Change (IPCC) is the United Nations body for assessing the science related to climate change.

iv   The World Economic Forum Annual Meeting, held in Davos-Klosters, Switzerland, at the beginning of the calendar year.

v   The 2019 United Nations Climate Action Summit, the 25th Conference of the Parties to the United Nations Framework Convention on Climate Change (COP25), held in Chile, 2–13 December 2019.

Sources and Permissions

1   David Crouch, "The Swedish 15-year-old who's cutting class to fight the climate crisis", *The Guardian*, 1 September 2018, https://www. theguardian.com/science/2018/sep/01/swedish-15-year-old-cutting-class-to-fight-the-climate-crisis.

2   Bengt Lindström, meteorologist, SMHI (Swedish Meteorological and Hydrological Institute), SVT (Sveriges Television AB), 22 July 2018, https://www.svt.se/nyheter/inrikes/smhi-varmaste-juli-pa-minst-260-ar-1.

3   "Greta Thunberg: "Vi vet – och vi kan göra något nu," *Svenska Dagbladet*, 31 May 2018, https://www.svd.se/vi-vet--och-vi-kan-gora-nagot-nu.

4   David Crouch, "The Swedish 15-year-old who's cutting class to fight the climate crisis", *The Guardian*, 1 September 2018, https://www. theguardian.com/science/2018/sep/01/swedish-15-year-old-cutting-class-to-fight-the-climate-crisis.

5   Greta Thunberg, "I will go on with the school strike," Instagram, 8 September 2018, https://www.instagram.com/p/Bnd3AG_hQEa/.

6   Myles Allen, Mustafa Babiker, Yang Chen, Heleen De Coninck, Sarah Connors, Renee van Diemen, Opha Pauline Dube, et al., *Global Warming of 1.5°C*, United Nations Intergovernmental Panel on Climate Change, 2018, https://www.ipcc.ch/sr15/.

7   "7.6 million people demand action after week of climate strikes", 350.org, 28 September 2019, https://350.org/7-million-people-demand-action-after-week-of-climate-strikes/.

8   Stuart McGurk, 'Greta Thunberg: "To do your best is no longer good enough"', *GQ*, copyright © The Condé Nast Publications Ltd, 12 August 2019, https://www.gq-magazine.co.uk/men-of-the-year/article/greta-thunberg-interview.

9   According to the Intergovernmental Panel on Climate Change (IPCC) special report *Global Warming of 1.5°C*, Chapter 2: Mitigation Pathways Compatible with 1.5°C in the Context of Sustainable Development, p. 101, https://www.ipcc.ch/sr15/chapter/spm/.

10 Ibid, p. 108.

11 According to the IPCC special report *Global Warming of 1.5°C*, Summary for Policymakers, p. 14, https://www.ipcc.ch/site/assets/uploads/sites/2/2019/05/SR15_SPM_version_report_LR.pdf.

12 Ibid, pp. 106–7.

13 Bengt Lindström, meteorologist, SMHI (Swedish Meteorological and Hydrological Institute), SVT (Sveriges Television AB), 22 July 2018, https://www.svt.se/nyheter/inrikes/smhi-varmaste-juli-pa-minst-260-ar-1.

14 "7.6 million people demand action after week of climate strikes", 350.org, 28 September 2019, https://350.org/7-million-people-demand-action-after-week-of-climate-strikes/.

The publisher is grateful for literary permissions to reproduce items subject to copyright which have been used with permission. Every effort has been made to trace the copyright holders and the publisher apologizes for any unintentional omission. We would be pleased to hear from any not acknowledged here and undertake to make all reasonable efforts to include the appropriate acknowledgement in any subsequent edition.

Pages 6, 22, 61: Address to the European Economic and Social Committee at Civil Society for rEUnaissance, 21 February 2019, used with permission; page 13: Greta Thunberg, "I will go on with the school strike", Instagram, 8 September 2018; page 16: Stuart McGurk, 'Greta Thunberg: "To do your best is no longer good enough"', *GQ*, copyright © The Condé Nast Publications Ltd, 12 August 2019, https://www.gq-magazine.co.uk/men-of-the-year/article/greta-thunberg-interview; pages 17, 36, 45: "The disarming case to act right now on climate change", Greta Thunberg, TED2018, to watch the full talk visit TED.com; pages 19–21, 24–27: address to the United States Congress, September 2019, originally published in *The Independent*; pages 52, 55–57, 60: a speech at the World Economic Forum Annual Meeting, Davos-Klosters, Switzerland, January 2019; pages 67–68: *Nelson Mandela by Himself: The Authorised Book of Quotations* edited by Sello Hatang and Sahm Venter (Pan Macmillan: Johannesburg, South Africa, 2017), copyright © 2011 Nelson R. Mandela and the Nelson Mandela Foundation, used by permission of the Nelson Mandela Foundation, Johannesburg, South Africa.